Energetic Evelyn and the Shiny Yellow Spots

Copyright © 2020 Yvonne Breiner
All rights reserved
First Edition

PAGE PUBLISHING, INC.
Conneaut Lake, PA

First originally published by Page Publishing 2020

ISBN 978-1-64701-123-9 (pbk)
ISBN 978-1-64701-125-3 (hc)
ISBN 978-1-64701-124-6 (digital)

Printed in the United States of America

Energetic Evelyn
and the
Shiny Yellow Spots

Written by
Yvonne Breiner

Illustrated by
Frank Passaretti

One beautiful, bright, sunny Sunday morning, in the front yard under the evergreen tree, two shivering sleepy bunnies were yearning for sunlight when…

"I hear you," whispered Energetic Evelyn.

"I'm over yonder," replied Tricky Treats.

Energetic Evelyn sprang out from under the evergreen tree and was instantly warmed by the heat of the shimmering sun. Peering over her shoulder, Energetic Evelyn said, "What happened? Why do you look so somber, Tricky Treats?"

Tricky Treats sauntered over the lush green lawn and softly replied, "Well, last night I overheard Rowdy Richard and Furry Freddie yapping about going to a birthday bunny bash for Curious Clara's second 'bunnyday.' They were extremely excited and planning great games to play with the bunnygoers."

"That sounds like a lot of fun," said Energetic Evelyn. "So why are you so gloomy and glum?"

Tricky Treats slowly sat down on the plush green grass and grumbled, "I wasn't invited to the party, and…I think I know why!"

"Now, now," Energetic Evelyn gently said, "try to be positive and not so negative… Together, we will burrow to the bottom of this."

Tricky Treats tried to smile and said, "I truly try to be as positive as I possibly can. I know I 'look' definitely different from the other bunnies, seeing that I have yellow spots scattered on my bushy back. I know I stand out from all the other bunnies… I don't 'blend' in like the other happy hares."

"Who said that you had to 'blend' in with all the others?" Energetic Evelyn asked.

Tricky Treats softly replied, "From when I was a baby bunny, I have always loved the color of my furry fur. I loved my unique yellow color that, during the day, shone like the shimmering sun and then glistened in the sunset. I always felt proud of my color 'difference' until last year, when I was told how 'different' I really was. Now I just want to roll in the luscious green grass and erase all of my yellow spots. I want to simply be the 'same' as every other bunny!"

Energetic Evelyn exclaimed, "Okay, Tricky Treats, if that is what you truly, truly, truly want—to be simply the *same* as every other bunny."

As Tricky Treats peered into Energetic Evelyn's heavenly hazel eyes, he could tell that she did not agree with his choice to try to be the "same" as everyone else. He could sense the disappointment in Energetic Evelyn's eyes.

Energetic Evelyn cautioned, "You must make choices that you can live with, Tricky Treats. You can only make yourself happy and be content with what you call your 'differences,' but I don't see it that way."

Tricky Treats suddenly interrupted Energetic Evelyn and exclaimed, "I want to fit in with everyone else, I want to go to parties, I want to have furry friends, I want to hop happily along like every other bunny. *Wait*… That is a lot of *I*s, isn't it?"

Calmly, Energetic Evelyn replied, "Yes, it is! And by the way, what is stopping you from fitting in? Think about it. Just be yourself, and your true furry friends will see the real rabbit inside of you."

Tricky Treats blurted out, "I am unique, different, an individual, and a brave little bunny. I truly, truly, truly feel I can make a difference. I will make yellow spots the new normal. I am going to change the bunnies' attitudes and make the bunny world a wonderful place to hop in. I am going to stand up for myself and all bunnies that are different and unique."

Tricky Treats hopped around with confidence and decided he would boldly speak to the other bunnies about including all "unique" animals and accepting everyone as they are!

Tricky Treats

You're Invited!

"What a day this has been." Tricky Treats sighed as he hopped home, only to find the invitation to the birthday party in his round rabbit hole.

The End

About the Author

Yvonne is an elementary school teacher in New Jersey. She is the youngest of seven children and was born and raised in the small town of Suffield, Ohio. Ever since Yvonne was a child, she was sensitive to bullying and always was empathetic to the person being bullied.

She loves to write and based this story on her late mother, Evelyn Shilts. Evelyn was a kind, caring, considerate, giving, generous, accepting, nonjudgmental mother of seven. Evelyn loved her family, her husband, and was the most unselfish person in all regards. She loved bunnies and the gentle way they took care of their young and one another, which was the inspiration for *Energetic Evelyn and the Shiny Yellow Spots*.

Additionally, Yvonne loves to compose poetry, write stories, read, travel, walk in the park, complete crossword puzzles, and play cards. She especially cherishes spending time with her husband Freddie, family and friends. Yvonne feels blessed to have the ultimate job—teaching. She is extremely proud of this book and hopes all those that read it will see the moral and educational value gained by accepting others just the way they *are*.

Yvonne has always encouraged her students to persevere, "Dream Big," and to treat others as they would like to be treated. A portion of the sales of this book will be donated to the Lewy Body Dementia Assoc., which is the disease from which Evelyn suffered. Evelyn was courageous in the way she fought this disease while never wavering from her gentle demeanor and love of her family.

CPSIA information can be obtained
at www.ICGtesting.com
Printed in the USA
BVHW022240050820
585658BV00016B/79